This book belongs to:

Test Your Colors Here

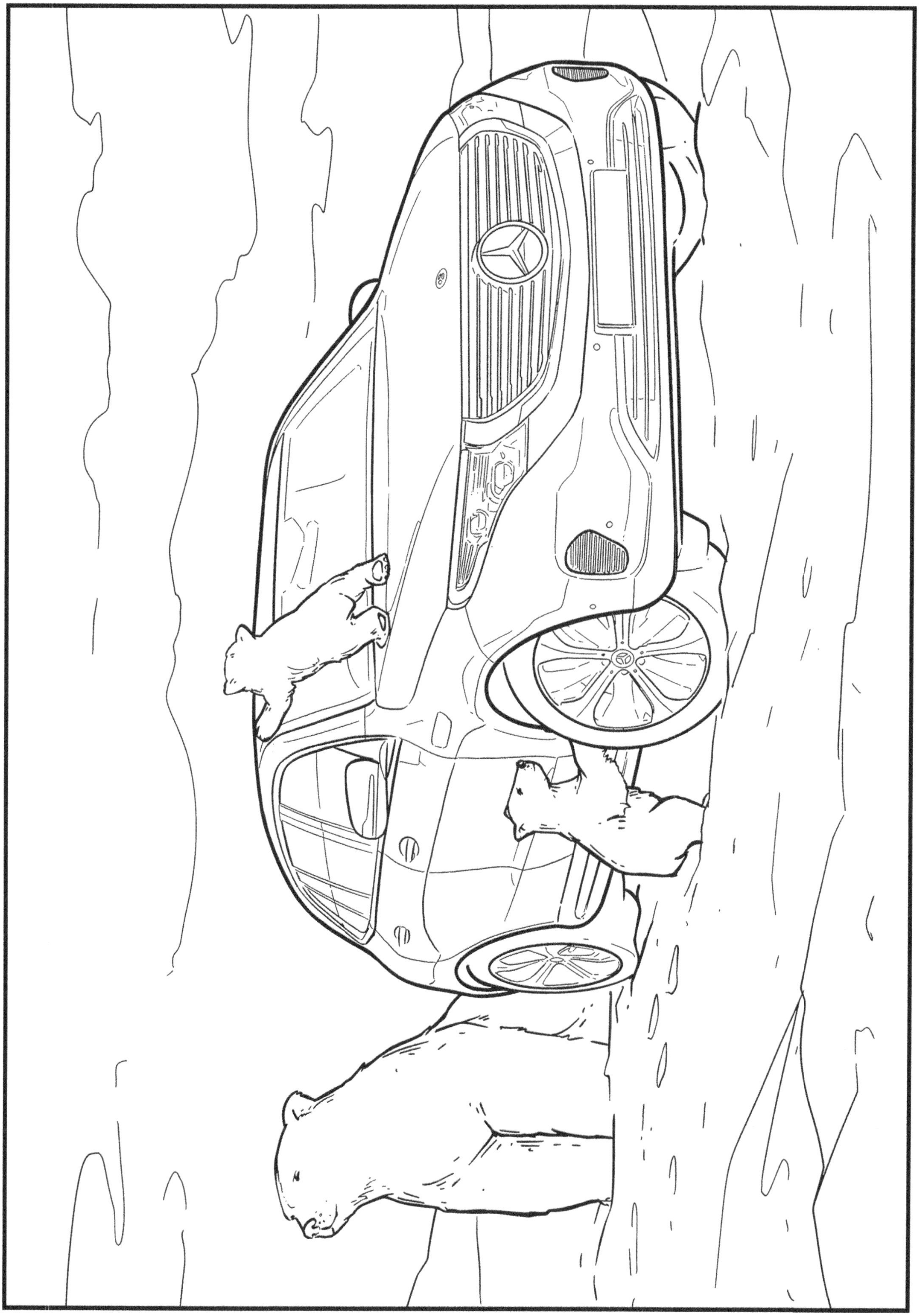

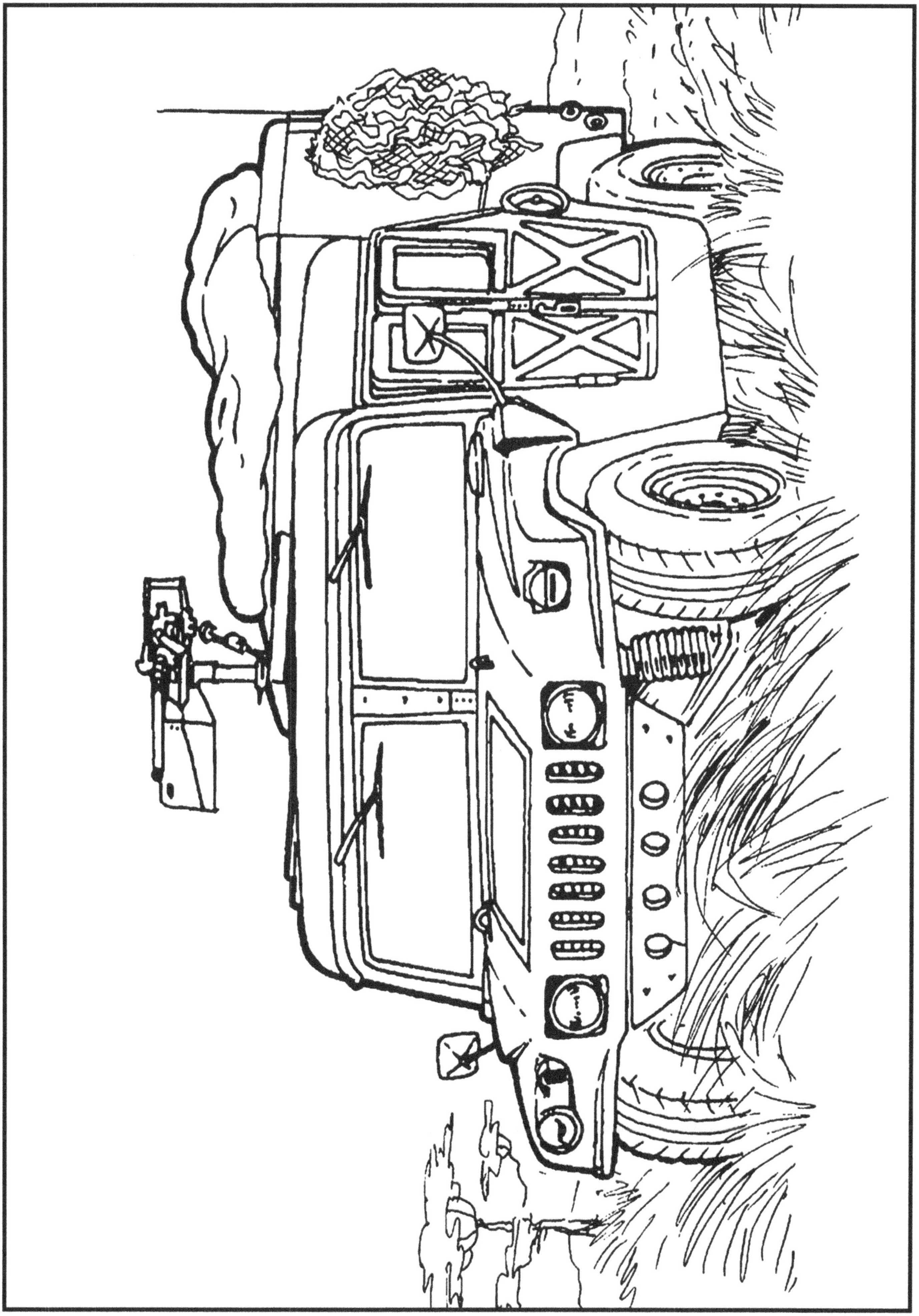

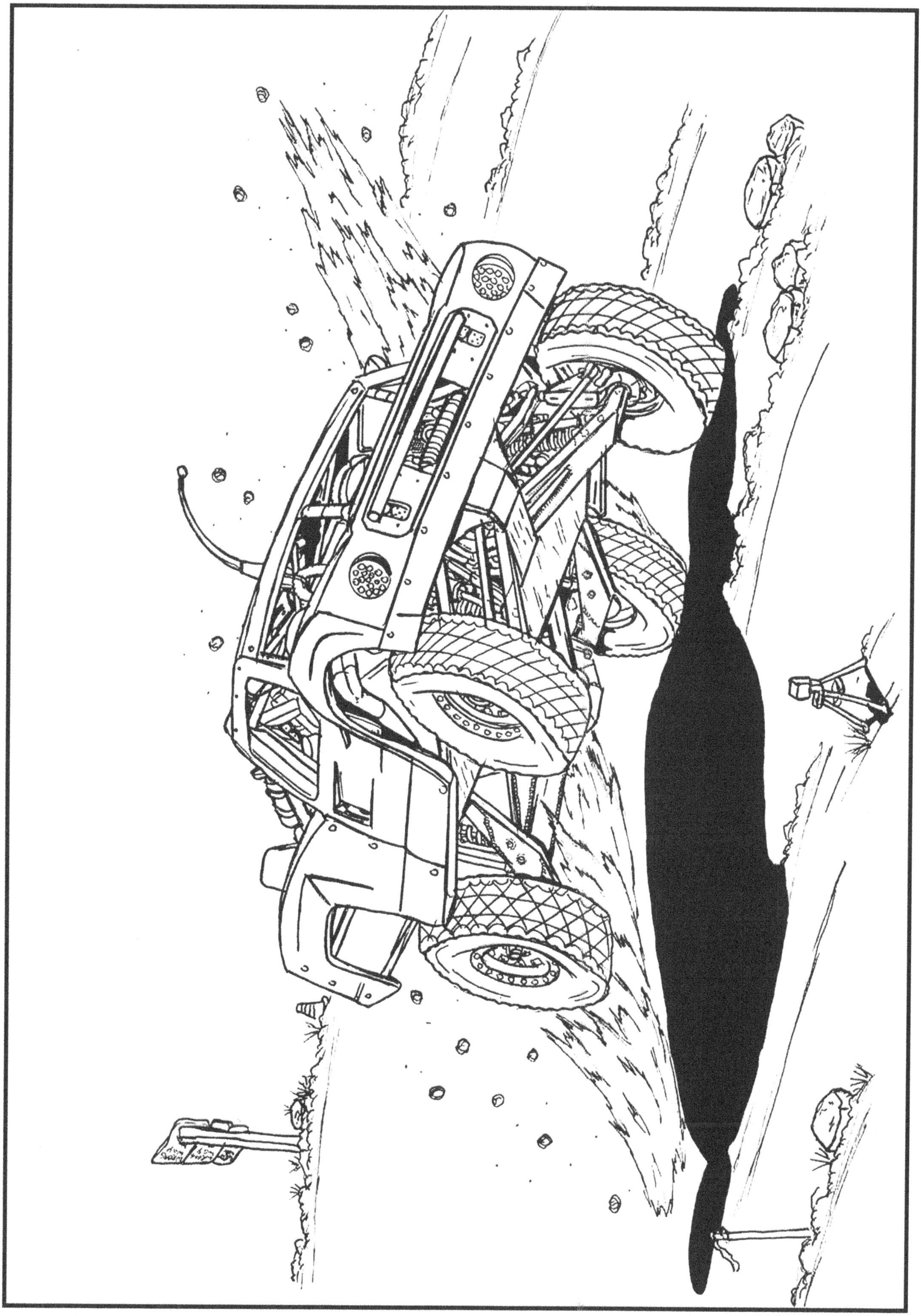

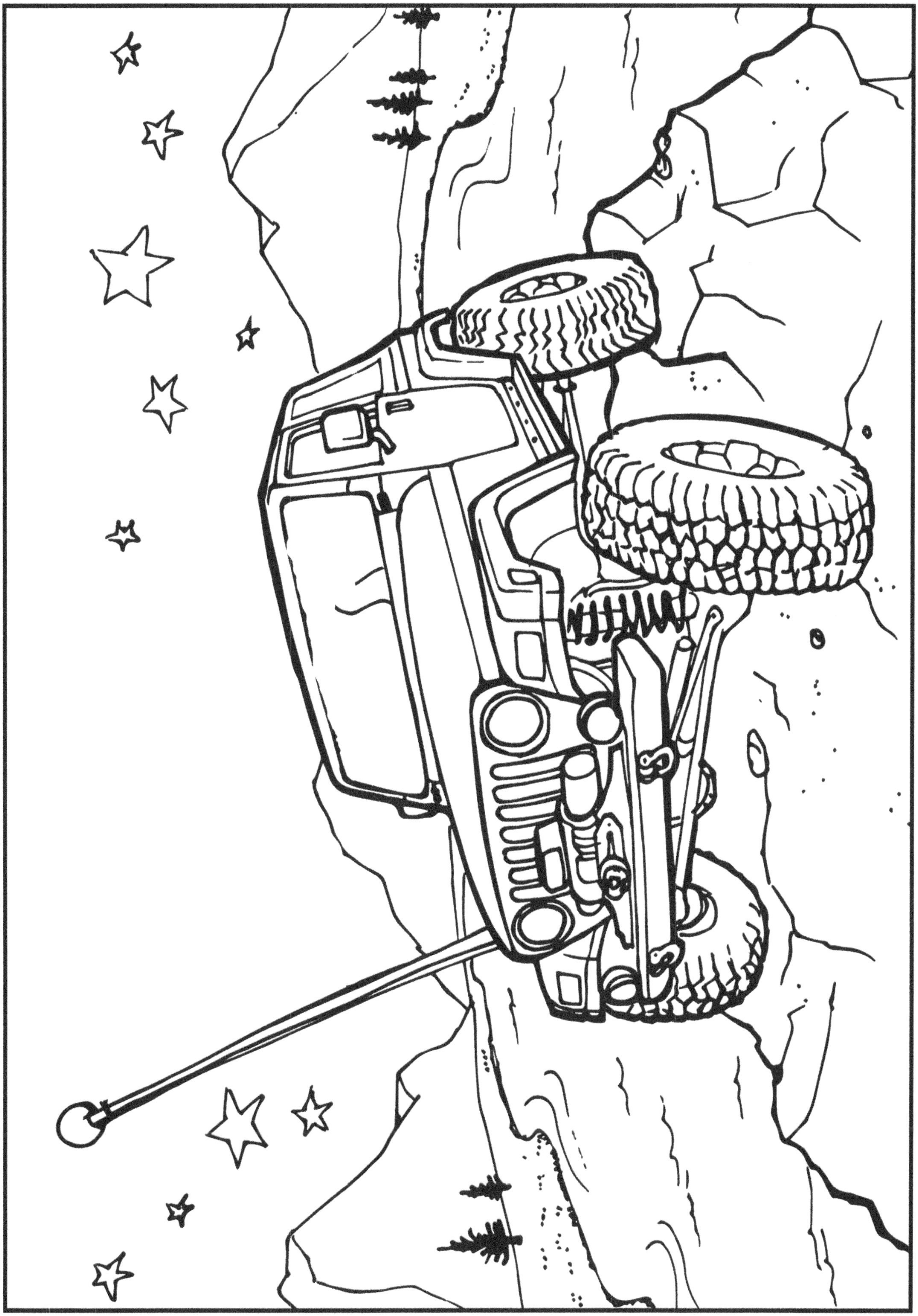

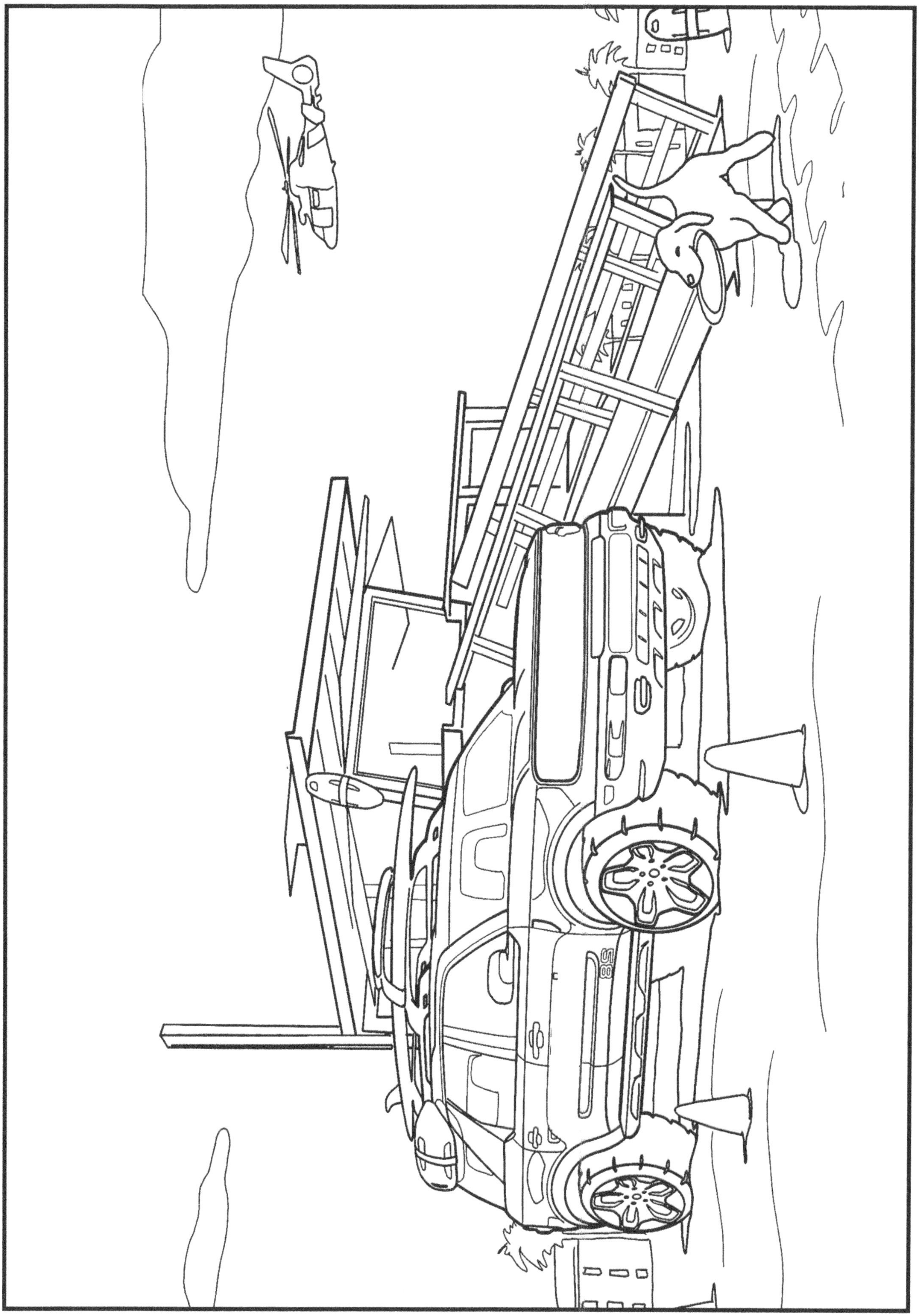

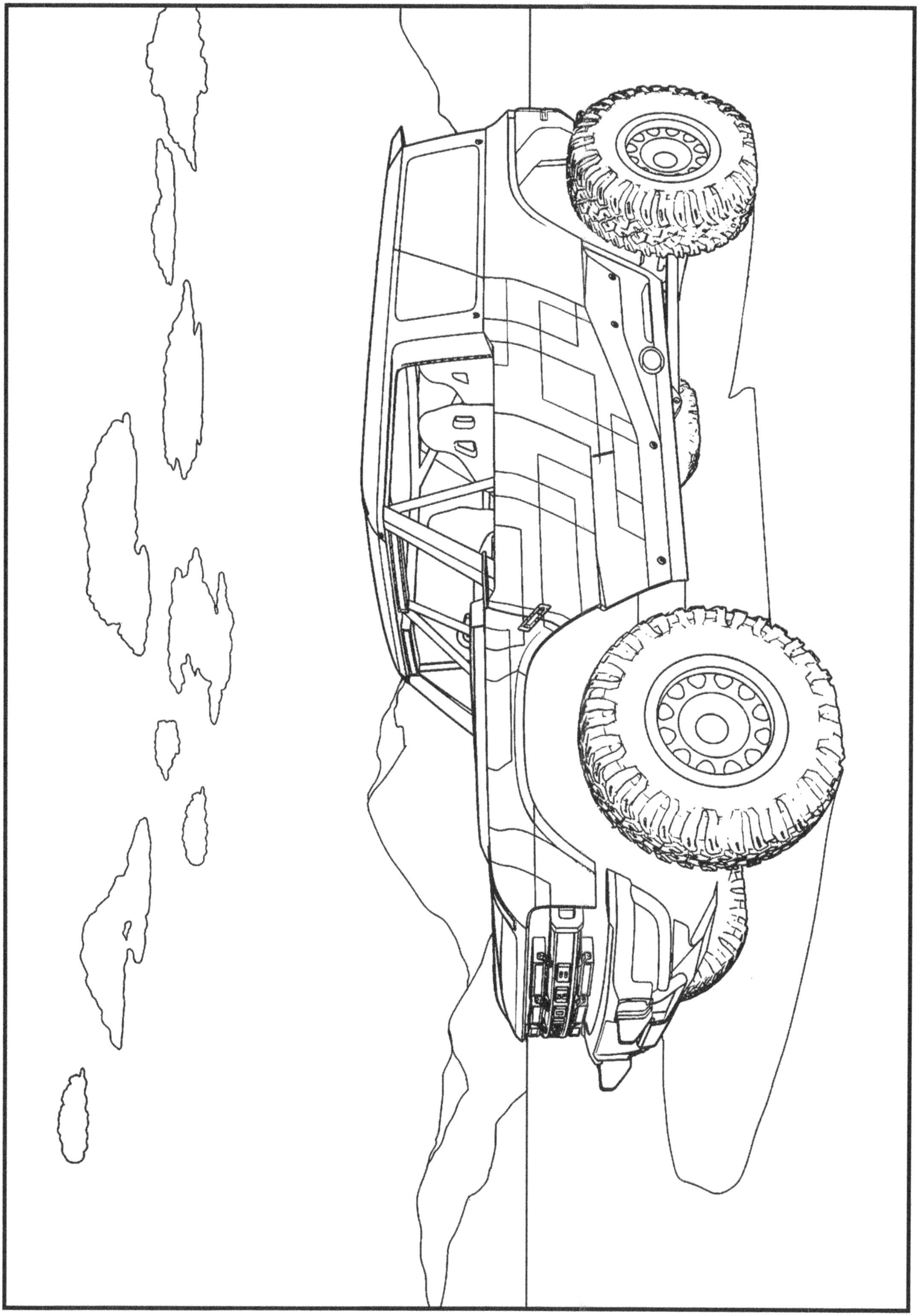

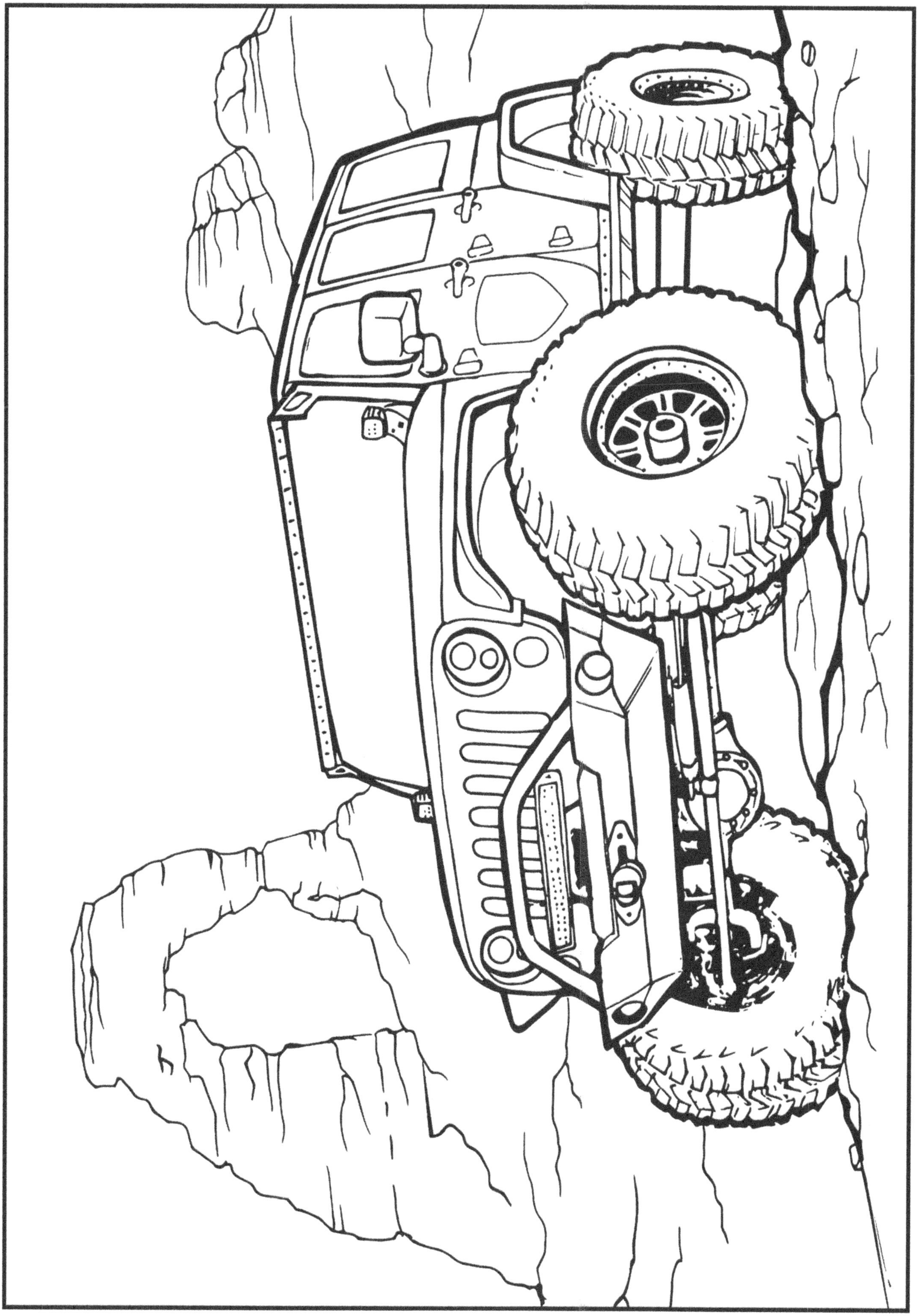

TERAFLEX

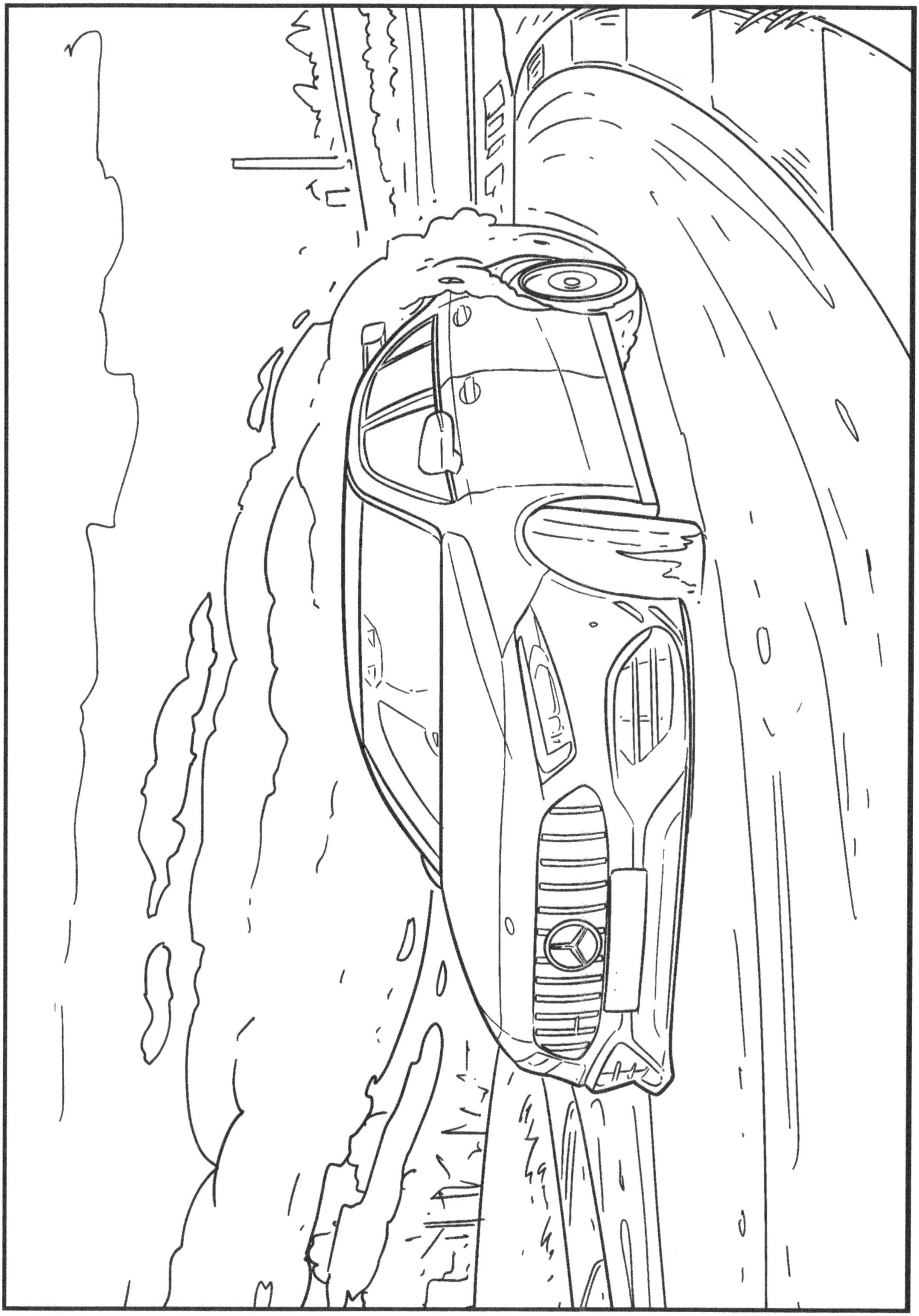

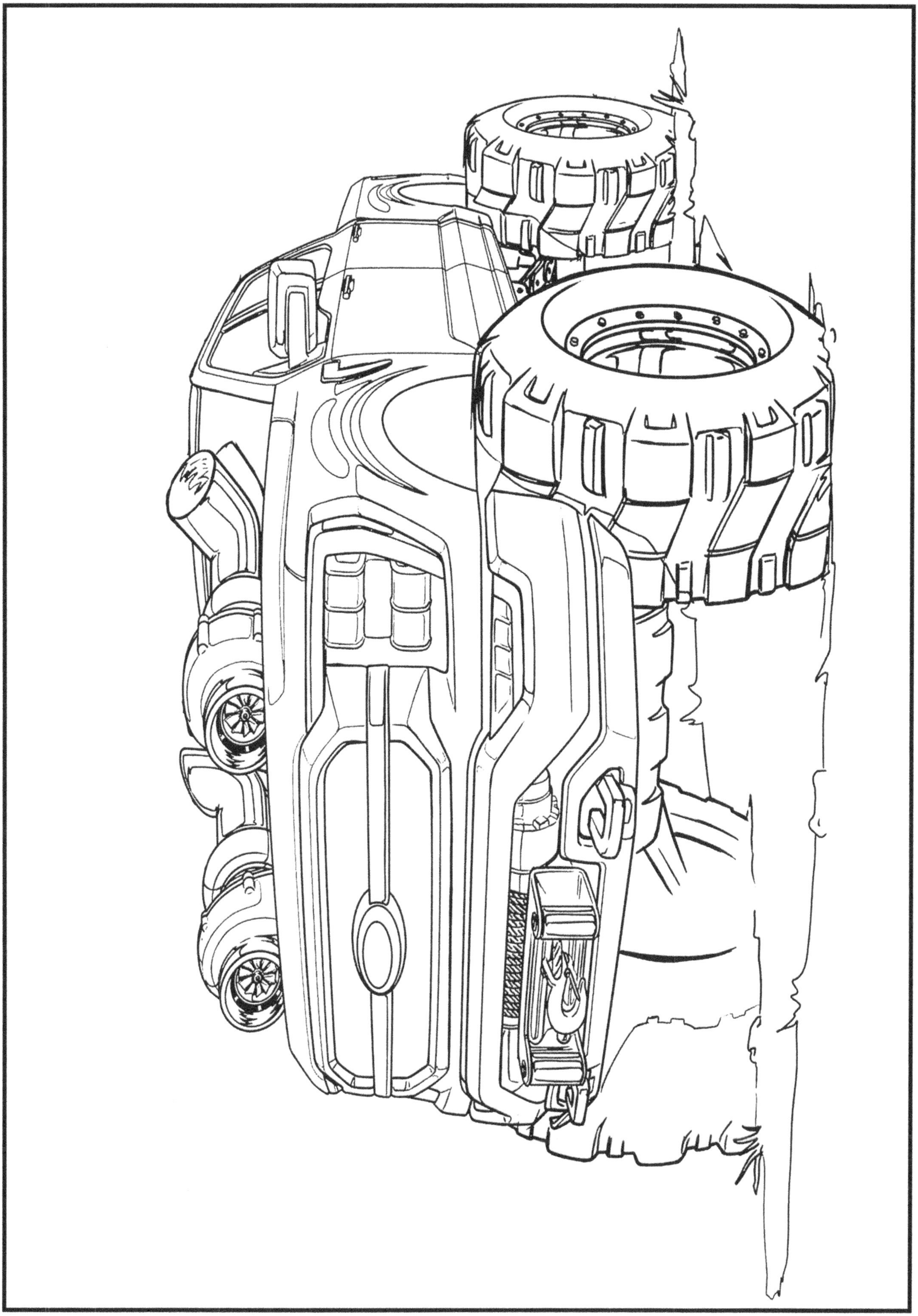

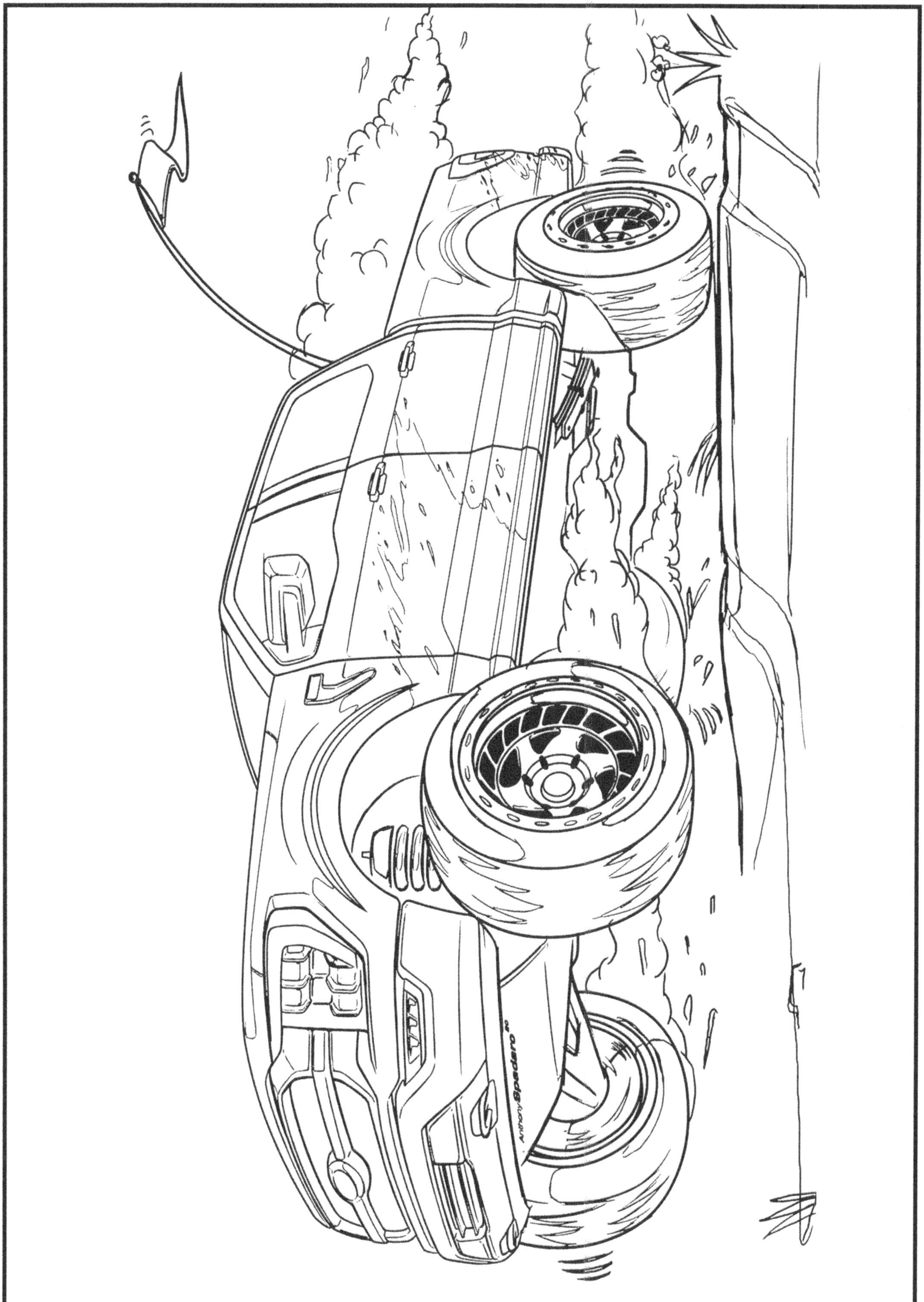
Anthony Spadaro

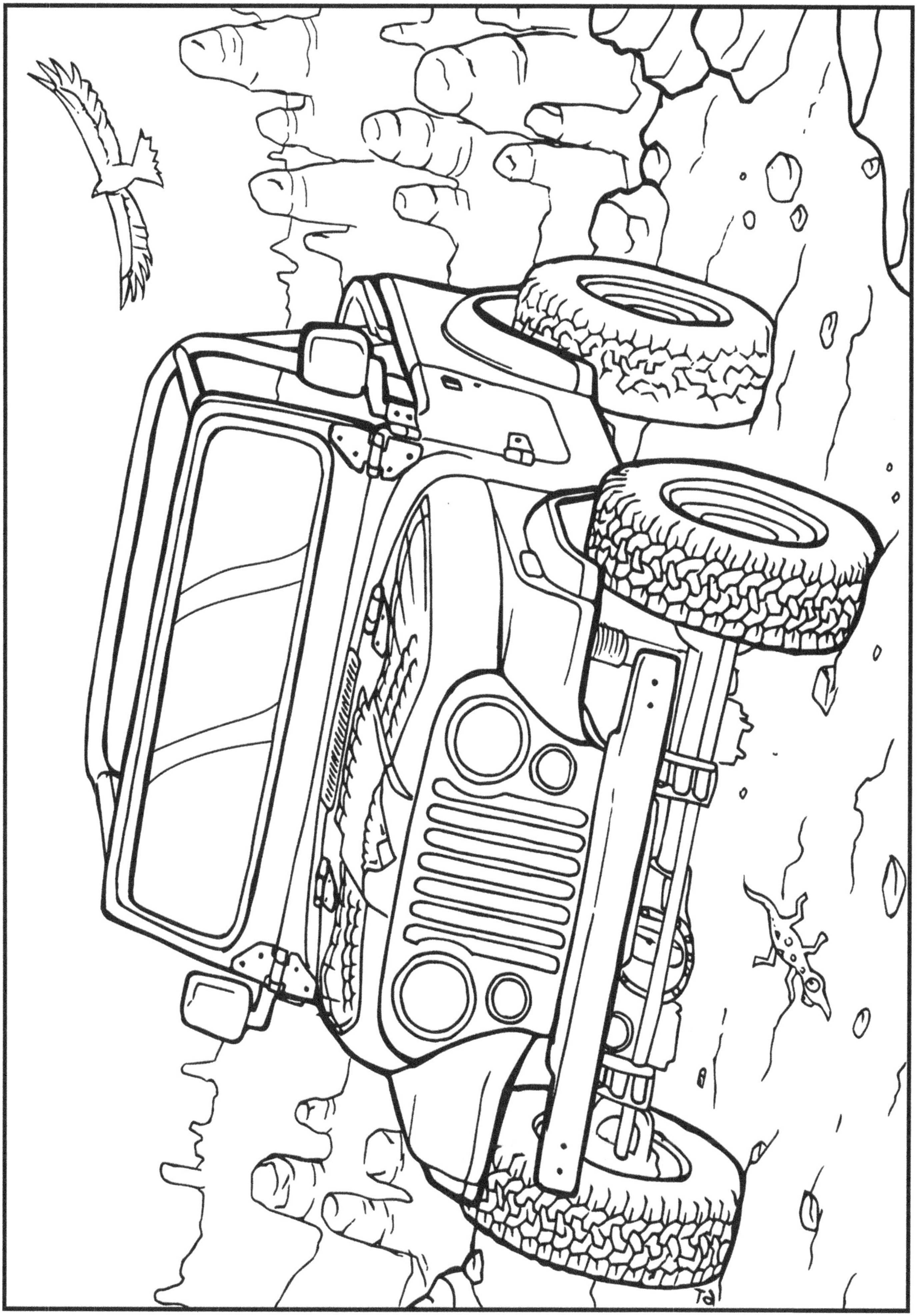

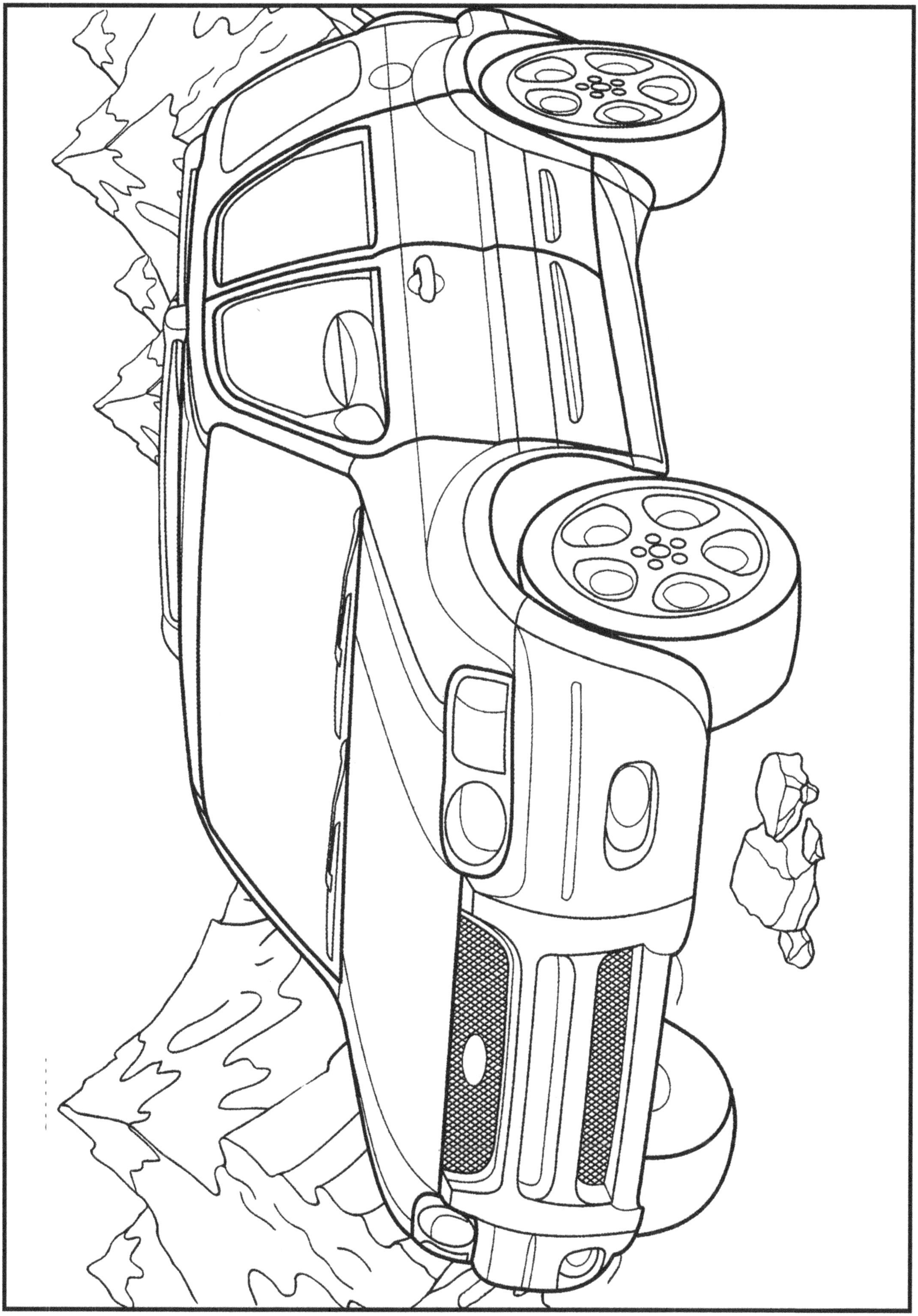

Made in the USA
Coppell, TX
01 February 2024

28448722R00031